What Do We Know About the Giant's Causeway?

by Ken Wright

illustrated by Andrew Thomson

Penguin Workshop

For Paula, Francesco, and Lock—KW

For Rhia, Cerys, and Esme—AT

PENGUIN WORKSHOP
An imprint of Penguin Random House LLC
1745 Broadway, New York, NY 10019
penguinrandomhouse.com

Library of Congress Cataloging-in-Publication Data is available.

First published in the United States of America by Penguin Workshop, 2026

Manufactured in the United States of America
CJKW

ISBN 9798217050994 (paperback)
10 9 8 7 6 5 4 3 2 1

ISBN 9798217051007 (library binding)
10 9 8 7 6 5 4 3 2 1

The authorized representative in the EU for product safety and compliance is Penguin Random House Ireland, Morrison Chambers, 32 Nassau Street, Dublin D02 YH68, Ireland, https://eu-contact.penguin.ie.

Contents

What Do We Know About the Giant's Causeway?

On a November day in 2015, a video circulated in a small area of Northern Ireland. It appeared to be a breaking news report about a giant that had been seen roaming nearby. The speaker on the video explained that a tourist had used their phone to take some video footage showing an enormous cave door opening and then quickly shutting tight.

He said that the giant that had been spotted earlier had probably entered the cave for his long winter hibernation. Tourists in the area that day were even said to have heard loud snoring coming from the cave. The video immediately caught the attention of people in this remote part of the country. They must have wondered if what they'd seen and heard could possibly be true. But how could they have even imagined that it would be?

About sixty miles northwest of Belfast, the capital of Northern Ireland, is County Antrim. It sits along the rugged, inhospitable, and sparsely populated coast of the North Atlantic Ocean. Yet, County Antrim is world famous. About seven hundred thousand people make the trip there each year to see one of the greatest wonders in the United Kingdom—an enormous collection of rocks and stones that are the stuff of history, wonder, and mystery.

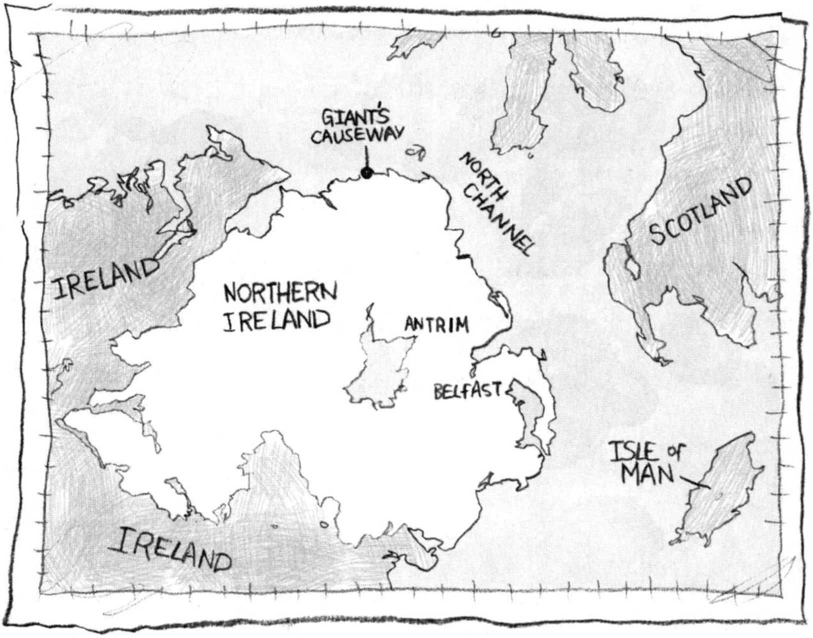

At the edge of this area of Northern Ireland, where the rocky coast looks out over the icy waters, an enormous collection of thousands of dark brown uniform stone columns rises out of the cliffs and descends into the cold, choppy Atlantic. Most people's first impression is that it looks like a gigantic staircase. Known today as the Giant's Causeway, this magnificent place has captivated people's imaginations for centuries.

Its amazing beauty is one reason, of course. But just as remarkable are the stories of how it came to be in the first place.

Did a giant build a causeway here to get across the sea to an island in Scotland, eighty-two miles away? Ancient stories and folklore tell us just

that. And its name—Giant's Causeway—certainly suggests it. (A causeway is a raised rocky path or road built across a body of water or wet, marshy land. It is different from a bridge, which is built suspended above a gap, such as a river, valley, or another road, with open space below it.)

Or are there more natural causes for its origin, ones that maybe science can explain? To this day, nobody knows for sure if giants once lived among the rocks and towering cliffs that make up the Giant's Causeway. Nor can we be sure if one might still live there today.

Could the video provide some proof that the stories people have told for centuries might be true? Or is the idea of a giant existing here impossible to believe?

CHAPTER 1
Where Giants Roam

The first people to see the Giant's Causeway arrived in Ireland around nine thousand years ago. Archaeologists have discovered a few traces of human existence in the area going back that far.

(An archaeologist is someone who digs up and studies the things that early people made and used in daily life.) But these archaeologists do not know enough to say for sure who these people were or how they lived.

There is much more evidence of people living

there later in history. Settlement sites and artifacts such as tools and weapons dating back five thousand years have been dug up by archaeologists. And the evidence of human settlements grows even greater as times goes on, into the 900s CE, and all the way through to the 1400s and later.

Many people have set eyes on the causeway over time. They most likely had different impressions of what it was, especially if they thought it looked like huge stepping stones leading to the cliffs above and the waters below.

They probably told stories about what they saw. But we will never know for certain. That's because no written evidence from those times has been discovered. Not a single description or impression of the Giant's Causeway has come down to us from all those years ago.

While there are no written records, we are pretty sure that the Giant's Causeway must have been a special place for these ancient people. Stories of early Irish warriors and heroes were being told orally (meaning spoken, not written) as early as 100 CE. As far as we know, these were not written down at the time. That would not happen until many years later. But it is from those stories, a rich trove of Irish myths and legends that were eventually written down and passed down to us hundreds of years later, that we start to get an understanding of what the early Irish people might have thought of the Giant's Causeway and the surrounding area.

We know that long before the Giant's Causeway got its now well-known name, it had an ancient Irish name: *Clochan na bhFomharaigh* (say: KLO-kawn na VOH-vor-ukh). In English this means "the stepping stones of the Fomorians." In Irish mythology, the Fomorians were often portrayed as giant, monstrous creatures, some with the bodies of humans and the heads of goats, and others with human heads but just one eye in the middle of the forehead!

The Shanachie

The oral tradition of Irish storytelling is thousands of years old. During the time when most people could not read or write, oral (nonwritten) storytelling was the main way for information, history, and entertainment to be remembered and passed along. A traditional Irish storyteller, often known as a "shanachie" (say: SHAN-e-khee)—meaning "bearer of old lore"—would travel from village to village to bring news to the local people. A shanachie was an important, trusted person in early Irish society. The stories they told, in poetry and song, were considered by the public as historically authentic and accurate.

A shanachie told a wide range of stories. Local news, information, and history were themes that they regularly covered. But the most appealing and unforgettable stories were the tales of magic, nature, and adventure that included the exploits of kings and queens, warriors and heroes, and, yes, giants.

We will probably never know exactly what the Fomorians looked like. But their name for the Giant's Causeway tells us something about their idea of it as a place where giants could certainly have roamed. It just might give us a clue about who may have built it!

Stories like this and many others were eventually written down (thousands of years later) in collections known today as the Four Cycles of Irish Mythology. These cycles are the sources of our knowledge of the history, mythology, and lore of ancient Ireland.

Imagine the Four Cycles as chapters in one large storybook about the amazing history of Ireland and its brave, colorful, mysterious, and heroic characters.

CHAPTER 2
Discovery and Spreading the Word

We can only imagine what the ancient people of Ireland thought of the Giant's Causeway. But fast-forward many centuries, all the way to the year 1688, when the first known impression of the Giant's Causeway was finally put down in writing. It was written by Sir Robert Redding, a naturalist (a scientist who studies the natural world) and member of the scientific institution called the Royal Society, as a letter to other members of the society.

THE ROYAL SOCIETY

The Royal Society

The Royal Society is the world's oldest scientific academy. Founded in London, England, in 1660, its purpose was to bring together leading scientists from England and other countries to promote scientific awareness and discovery of the natural world, to debate new scientific ideas, and to share knowledge. For its first 285 years, the Society only allowed men as members. It was not until 1945 that women scientists were admitted.

Still in existence today, the Royal Society is one of the leading academic institutions in the world, continuing to promote and support excellence in the pursuit of science.

THE ROYAL SOCIETY
2
7

It provides a very short description of the giant rock formation. While we know that Redding traveled to the north of Ireland at the time the letter was written, there is no actual evidence that he visited the site. He may have seen it for himself. He may have heard the description from someone he met on his trip who described it to him. We just don't know. But we have his words, the first ones we know to be written down about the Giant's Causeway.

Sir Robert wrote: "Description of ye Giants Causey within 2 miles of Dunluce, to the north thereof, in the county of Antrim in Ireland, where there are a vast quantity of Hexagonall Pillars of stone about 8 Inches wide, which stand pitch't perpendicularly as in a Pavement running down obliquely into the Sea. These columns are so regularly ranged and fitted one to the other that it seems rather the work of art than nature . . ."

Redding's last line—"These columns are so regularly ranged and fitted one to the other that it seems rather the work of art than nature"—must have excited the curiosity of all those who read it! What he meant by it was that the stones looked as if they had been intentionally arranged that way, not randomly formed by nature.

News of Redding's letter quickly circulated at the Royal Society, and soon there was real interest by others at the Society to see the Giant's Causeway.

The relationship between Great Britain and Ireland changed and evolved over many years. By the 1600s, Britain had considerable political control over Ireland, and by the 1800s the two were officially united as one country called the United Kingdom.

Expeditions were organized to visit the north of Ireland. People traveled from as far away as London, in England, and from the cities of Dublin and Belfast in Ireland. Travel in Ireland in the 1600s was challenging and could be dangerous. These trips were especially difficult for travelers because the north of Ireland was still very remote. With rugged terrain and often uncharted roadways, there was little chance of an easy time of it. And there were very few accommodations once the travelers got there.

But these kinds of inconveniences did not deter the scientists and others who were determined to see these mysterious stone and rock formations for themselves. People making the trip to see the Giant's Causeway were very motivated to get there, so they took their chances!

The Bumpy Ride to the Giant's Causeway

Travel over land in Ireland in the 1600s was extremely difficult and very slow. There were few roads at the time, and those that existed were muddy and rough. Most of the people in this period who traveled to the Giant's Causeway would have gone by horse-drawn carts or carriages. The trip would never have been comfortable because of the inevitable bumpy ride and would take days to get there.

The distance between Belfast and the Giant's Causeway is only about sixty miles. But in the 1600s, the trip would take at least two long days and often more. From Dublin, where many of the travelers to the causeway originated their trip, it would take as many as five days to travel the 162-mile journey on those rough, uneven, and unpaved roads.

Of course, the trip itself was usually extremely uncomfortable. In addition, these intrepid travelers had to be on the lookout in such a rural and remote area for bandits and thieves, who might be waiting to relieve them of their money and valuables!

William King

Two of the first people we know of to travel to the causeway after Redding's letter appeared were William King, a bishop of Derry, a town in Northern Ireland, and a student at Cambridge University in England. The student was a friend of King's, but his name is not now known. This was in 1692, only four years after Redding's description circulated. The student wrote about their visit, and, like Redding, he sent his account to the Royal Society. It was King's and his student friend's accounts that then led Sir Richard Bulkeley, an Irish politician, to write the first-ever published description of the Giant's Causeway, in the *Philosophical Transactions of the Royal Society*, in 1693.

In the 1600s and 1700s, a person who first saw or discovered something in the natural world was not always the one to get credit for doing so. That distinction usually went to the person who actually published the news in an official paper. This was usually a wealthy man who could afford to publish his opinions and join established "societies." So, Sir Richard Bulkeley, not Sir Robert Redding, and not even William King, earned the honor of having "discovered" the Giant's Causeway. Redding's letter was never officially published. Today it doesn't really matter who got the credit. What's important is that

Sir Richard Bulkeley

with Bulkeley's published account, official word was finally out!

Once and for all, the world knew about the newly discovered Giant's Causeway. From then there was no stopping the number of people fascinated by what they read. They were eager to see what all the excitement was about. Scholars, scientists, naturalists, storytellers, and artists began making plans for the difficult trip to admire and study this new, mysterious place.

One of the most important people to help spread the word about the Giant's Causeway was an Irish artist named Susanna Drury. Very little is known about Drury, including when she was born or when she died. But we do know that in 1739 she traveled to the north of Ireland and stayed near the Giant's Causeway for three months. She created several paintings of the site, which were the first truly accurate images of the Giant's Causeway. These were large, full-color paintings, and they did more than anything at the time to inform the public about the existence of the causeway. Once these paintings became widely seen, they were often copied and published in books, spreading the word to even more people. Drury received an award for her paintings from the Dublin Society, an Irish charitable organization, in 1740. She was the first woman in Ireland to receive this award. Today Drury's paintings hang in the Ulster Museum in Belfast for everyone to see.

Drury's famous paintings may have inspired one of the most prominent women of her day to make the difficult trip to visit the Giant's Causeway. Mary Delany was an English artist, professional writer, and courtier (a companion to royalty) who was well-known by many of the most famous artists, authors, and musicians

Mary Delany

King George III and Queen Charlotte of England

of the day. She was even on friendly terms with King George III and Queen Charlotte of England!

Delany traveled to the Giant's Causeway in 1758 to see firsthand what everyone was so excited about. She wrote many letters about what she experienced and recorded many of her impressions of the Giant's Causeway in her diaries. Being an artist, she also sketched what

she saw. A collection of documents from her travels in Ireland was eventually published as a book called *Letters from Georgian Ireland*. (The Georgian era of British history is from 1714 to 1837, covering the reigns of King George I through King George IV.)

Mary Delany had a lot to say about her visit to the Giant's Causeway. After her first visit to the site, she wrote: "I know my dearest sister will want to know how we get out of the Giant's claws, and I must tell her we are just returned from seeing the most wonderful sight that, perhaps, is to be seen in the world . . ."

Delany's words echoed the stories that came before hers, as well as the awe and amazement that would come after.

CHAPTER 3
Stepping Stones to the Sea

"The most wonderful sight that, perhaps, is to be seen in the world" is actually made up of three parts—the Little, Middle, and Grand Causeways, and in total it stretches four miles along the Antrim coast, covering a total of 173 acres.

Middle Causeway

That is huge—comparable to 131 football fields or 2,684 tennis courts! Its cliffs soar to 330 feet at their highest. Its most remarkable feature is a collection of approximately forty thousand interconnected stone columns. Most of these are hexagonal (six-sided) in shape, between fifteen and twenty inches wide, the tallest rising to about forty feet high—that's about the height of an average four-story building. The overall effect is similar to seeing forty thousand yellow school buses upended and stacked closely together!

The general impression many people have when they first see these columns is that they seem to be made up of exactly similar parts, as if they are too perfect to be a natural formation. In fact, the sense many visitors have when touring the site is that the causeway actually looks human-made—or giant-made—with enormous and precisely designed stepping stones leading down to the waters below.

So, is this place too perfect to be a natural formation? It does appear that way. And if that's the case, then who could have created such a place if not Mother Nature?

Keen observers will tell us that there are obvious signs across the entire causeway. For example, near the Little Causeway there is a collection of large, rounded stones that are scattered around as if they were left behind after being played with. These are not called the Giant's Marbles for nothing! There are many more signs if the curious and imaginative visitor looks closely.

Giant's Marbles

At the Grand Causeway, there is a group of stones that are perfectly shaped to resemble an enormous handheld fan, the type of fan a very large person would use to cool themselves in warm weather. Locals and others are so sure of its origin that it has been dubbed the Giant's Fan.

Giant's Fan

And if these are not enough signs to point us in the direction of giant creators, there is one very popular formation that just might clinch it! Way below the cliffs, down near the edge of the water, is a large object in the exact shape of a person's boot—a very big boot that could only have belonged to a very big person! Measured by today's shoe sizes, the boot is believed to be a size 93½! Compared to the average shoe size of an eleven-year-old kid, which can be anywhere from size 3 to size 7, that's astonishing! People have calculated that a person with a size 93½ shoe would be about fifty-two feet tall!

What do all these clues tell us? Is this a place where giants really did roam, leaving their boots behind on the rocky shoreline?

CHAPTER 4
The Clash of Giants

Of all the characters in ancient Irish history and lore, none is more famous than Fionn mac Cumhaill (say: finn-m-COOL), commonly known as Finn McCool. Historians tell us that Finn was a warrior chieftain who lived in Ireland in the third century (200s) CE. The most famous tales of Finn's exploits appear in what is known as the Fenian Cycle, one of the four collections of stories about Irish history and mythology that have come down to us from ancient times. In it, Finn is a warrior of enormous strength and the leader of the Fenians, a standing army of what might have been between nine thousand and twenty thousand warrior soldiers. Finn was well-known for his strength and bravery. But legend also tells us he was known for being a giant. Some accounts say that Finn was at least fifty-two feet tall (and so could easily have had a 93½ shoe size!). Others say he was even taller! No one can know for sure just how big he was.

Fionn mac Cumhaill (Finn McCool)

Many stories about Finn's heroic accomplishments and wise leadership have been told throughout the centuries, but the most famous is about how he built the Giant's Causeway.

It is believed that Finn lived on the northeastern coast of Northern Ireland, where he fished the icy waters and tended to his flock of sheep on the hills above the cliffs. When he wasn't leading his warriors in battle, Finn and his wife, Oonagh, lived comfortably together there.

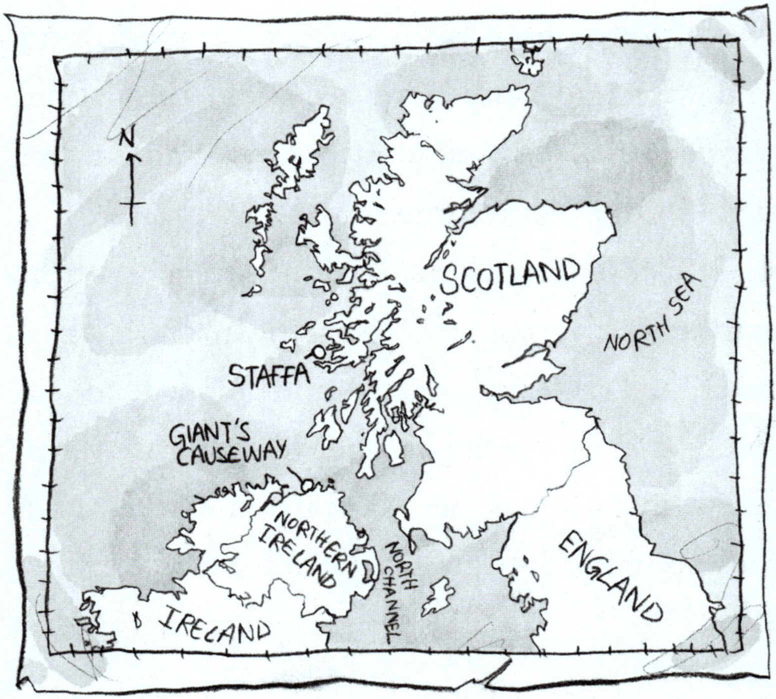

One version of the story is like this: On a bright, cold morning, Finn was down by the water, looking out across the sea while preparing for his day of fishing, when he heard a call from far away. Peering more closely out over the waters, Finn could just about see a tall figure standing on the cliffs of Staffa, a small Scottish island over eighty miles away. It was none other than Benandonner, the most powerful giant in all of Scotland. And what he heard from across the waters was Benandonner yelling insults and demanding to do battle with him. While Finn and Benandonner had never met in person, they were in fact great rivals. Stories about which of them was the biggest and fiercest giant had been told for many years.

On this cold morning, after hearing Benandonner call out to him, Finn decided it was time for the two of them to finally meet. He wanted to settle their rivalry once and for all. So, Finn accepted the challenge. Because there was no boat big enough to carry a giant across the sea, Finn decided to build—with his bare hands—a causeway all the way over to the island of Staffa, Benandonner's home. Using the huge stones that were scattered everywhere around the shoreline at the base of the cliffs, he began to work. This way, Benandonner could cross the water that separated them and make good on his challenge.

It took Finn a few days to build the immense causeway. Once it was finished, he waited and watched as the Scottish giant made his way across. But, when Benandonner drew near, Finn was terrified to see that his great rival was much larger than he ever imagined.

Benandonner looked even bigger, fiercer, and meaner than Finn! Scared for his life, Finn ran to his house, where he explained the frightening situation to Oonagh. As Benandonner approached the house, Oonagh had a quick and clever idea: dress Finn up as a baby!

Benandonner

Grabbing a blanket and a bonnet, Finn jumped into a box made to look like an enormous cradle. Oonagh told him to be quiet and pretend to sleep. Just then Benandonner arrived, pounding on the door and yelling out for Finn to come outside to fight him!

As Benandonner opened the door and stormed into the house, Oonagh pointed to the "baby" Finn and pleaded with Benandonner not to wake him. When Benandonner looked over at the disguised Finn lying in the cradle, it was his turn to be terrified. If Finn's baby was so gigantic, he thought, then Finn himself must be the biggest giant of all! Petrified and thinking Finn might return home at any moment, Benandonner ran as fast as he could out of the house and back across the causeway, destroying it as he went, stone by stone. He certainly did not want the fierce Finn to follow him home to Staffa.

While the causeway Finn had built between the north of Ireland and the Scottish island of Staffa was destroyed by Benandonner, the remains of Finn's feat of bravery and ingenuity still remain on both sides of it. On the Scottish island of Staffa, Benandonner's home, there is a site just as impressive in its own way as the Giant's Causeway.

Fingal's Cave

Fingal's Cave is believed to be at the other end of the long causeway that Finn McCool built. About eighty-two miles away, on Staffa, there are rock formations and hundreds of uniform stone columns exactly like those on the Irish side of the waterway known as the North Channel. They reach up to the cliffs from the shoreline in nearly an identical way. Fingal's Cave in Scotland even got its name from Finn. Fingal is believed to be the Scottish variation of the name Finn!

And many believe that this is the story of how the Giant's Causeway was made and how it got its name, and what is left of it today.

There are many tales of Finn McCool's amazing exploits. Building the Giant's Causeway is just one of them, and the most famous. But another story also involves his ongoing feud with the giant Benandonner. The Scottish giant had actually called Finn a coward and a "bonny wee bairn" (pretty little child)! One day, years before he built his causeway, Finn, in a fit of rage and tired of all the taunts and insults coming from the giant across the waters, grabbed a huge chunk of earth with his bare hands. He raised it far above his head and threw it as hard as he could at Benandonner, hoping to be done with his rival once and for all. But Finn seriously missed his target, by a long shot. The huge piece of earth landed smack in the middle of the Irish Sea instead.

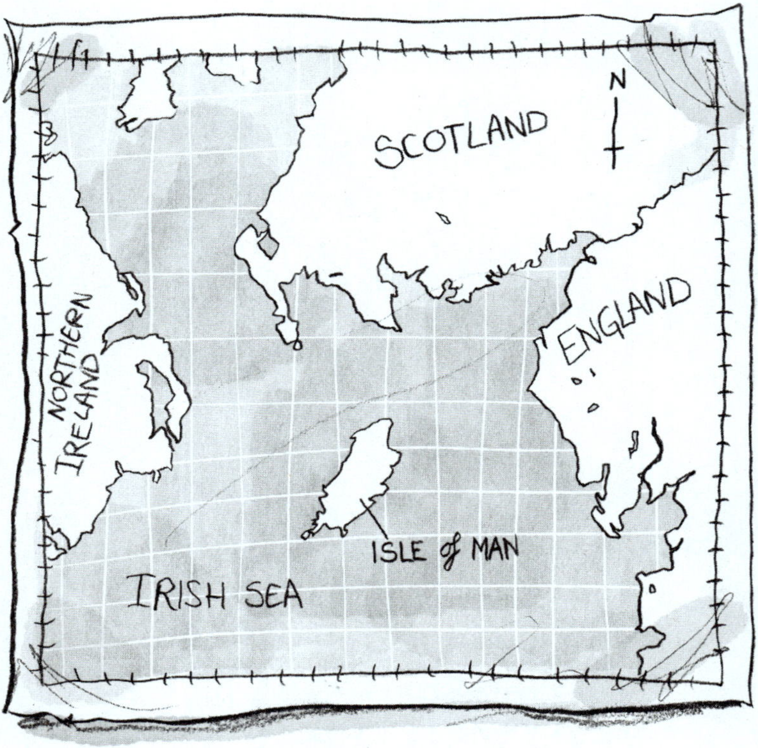

Isle of Man

This piece of earth was so big that it became an actual island right where it landed. That island is called the Isle of Man, and today it has a population of about eighty-four thousand people.

And what happened to the enormous hole

left behind in the ground after Finn pulled up that huge piece of earth? It became Lough Neagh, the largest lake on the island of Ireland and in all the United Kingdom. (*Lough* is the Irish word for *lake*.)

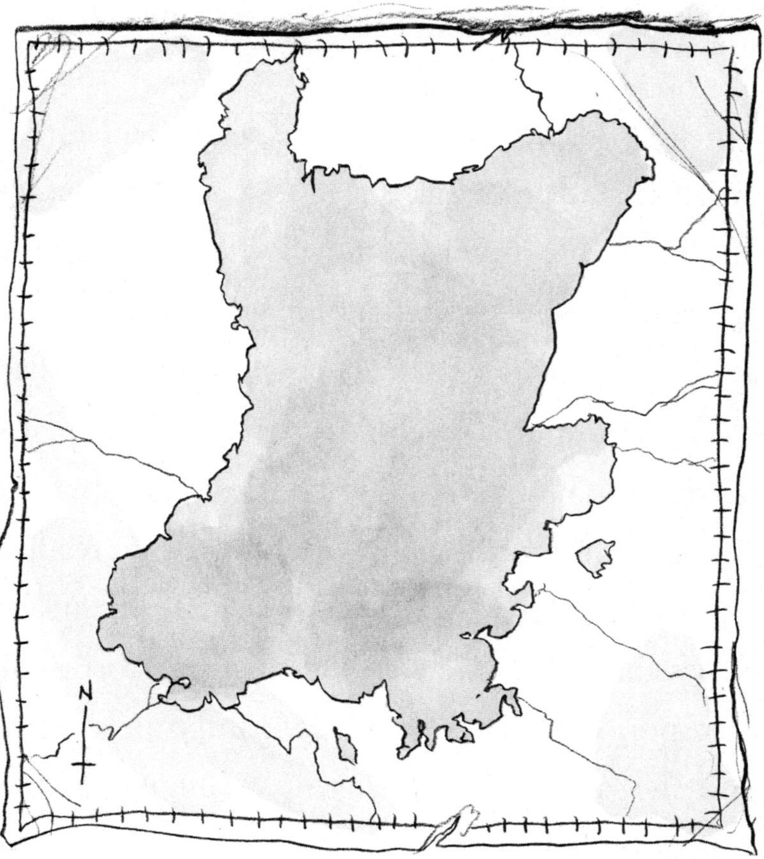

Lough Neagh

CHAPTER 5
Tourists, Guides, and Souvenirs

Beginning in the 1800s, knowledge of—and stories about—the Giant's Causeway spread very quickly. People from all over Ireland and Great Britain, and even as far away as continental Europe, were eager to travel there to see for themselves what all the fuss was about. As a result, enterprising local people realized that their community could be developed to accommodate the coming tourists. The people living in the shadow of the causeway readily expanded their businesses to fill the need. Accessible roads were built, different forms of transportation were introduced, and hotels, inns, and shops started to spring up as interest in the area exploded.

As tourists started to arrive in larger numbers, they were greeted by a growing number of guides—locals who lived in the villages along the nearby coast. The guides were more than ready to entertain tourists with fun facts about the surrounding area. And of course, they had stories about how the causeway may have been created—and by whom—to enrich the visitors' experiences of this mysterious place.

The Causeway Tram

Until the 1880s, the most reliable way for travelers to get to the Giant's Causeway was either by small boats (often treacherous) or by horse-drawn carriages (not very comfortable!). In the late 1800s, that all changed. Two enterprising brothers, Dr. William Traill, an engineer, and Dr. Anthony Traill, a scholar at Trinity College in Dublin, developed a new and exciting mode of transportation.

The Causeway Tram opened to the public in 1887. (A tram is a lot like what we know in the United States

as a streetcar or a trolley.) It became famous for being able to transport many more visitors than ever to the steep cliffs and columns of the causeway. Maybe even more important is that it was the first commercially run tram in the world to use hydroelectricity (the production of electricity by waterpower)!

Hailed as a marvel in its time, the Causeway Tram carried nearly sixty-five thousand people in its first year in operation to the site. The tram remained a reliable way for visitors to get to the site for more than sixty years. It was eventually replaced by a diesel train that operated along the same route.

Most of the guides were men, but women also took part in the work and shared their stories to educate and amuse. Many were working to earn money and make a living for their families. But they also became guides because they loved the site of the Giant's Causeway. And they loved the stories about it they had heard from their parents and grandparents growing up. They mixed facts and folklore to create the best stories possible, even changing details of the old stories for fun.

Their aim was to make the visitors laugh and wonder at the mystery of the place so that they would remember the stories and their visit to the Giant's Causeway.

Giant's Causeway tour guides in front of the visitors' center

At the top of the Middle Causeway, there is a large stone seat. Legend has it that the chair was made for Finn McCool when he was a child.

The Wishing Chair

The Wishing Chair is one of the most popular sites to see at the causeway because it is said that any wish made by people who sit in it will come true. Rumors have circulated for years that the giant Finn himself once made a wish while sitting in the chair. What was that wish? That he could one day build a causeway all the way to Scotland, of course!

Since then, other famous people have made the chair a must-see stop on their trip to the Giant's Causeway. Even King Charles III of England once visited when he was still the Prince of Wales. We can only guess what he wished for!

King Charles III, then Prince of Wales, at the wishing chair in 1996

Scattered across the causeway are signs of a giant's presence, and the guides made sure these were pointed out to the tourists and woven into their stories every chance they got.

To keep the mystery alive, who doesn't like a good story about giants?

In addition to acting as tour guides, locals also sold souvenirs to the throngs of tourists visiting each year. Women would walk along the rocks and columns of the causeway with cases of trinkets, postcards, pamphlets, and sometimes even rocks! They would tell stories of the giants who once roamed the area, hoping to make a sale or two. Later, stone carvings of the Wishing Chair became popular, as did a range of local crafts. The souvenir sellers at the Giant's Causeway became an important and colorful part of the experience of visits to the site.

CHAPTER 6
The Living Landscape of the Giant's Causeway

Wildlife at the Giant's Causeway is as plentiful as the stories about the giant who may have built it. And maybe just as famous! There are over fifty species of birds, two hundred species of plants, and hundreds of species of fish, insects, and mammals.

In the tall and rocky cliffs and along the rugged coastline that surround the causeway there are thousands of nooks and crannies that are perfect spots for birds to find food. This may seem an inhospitable place for people, but to the birds that make the causeway their home, it is a paradise.

Hovering in the skies over the causeway, landing on its cliffs or closer to the water to eat, rest, and nest are populations of razorbills, kittiwakes,

Razorbills

and fulmars. Fulmars look a lot like seagulls, but they are more closely related to another bird species, the albatross. They have a unique behavior. When defending their nest and chicks from would-be predators, they will spit out a disgusting-smelling liquid. So, approach at your own risk!

Albatross

Fulmars

Bird-watching is a popular activity at the causeway, and many birds that make their home there catch the attention of birders and tourists alike. The birds found there range from oystercatchers, who live along the shoreline, to buzzards and peregrine falcons, happy higher up near the top of the causeway. One very popular species of seabird to spot is the eider duck.

Eider ducks

Considered the biggest duck in the Northern Hemisphere, it is also the United Kingdom's heaviest and fastest-flying duck. Its habitat is also the nooks and crannies along the rocky coastline. While the eider ducks will not spit at you, it's always better if you view them and all wildlife from a distance, maybe with a good pair of binoculars.

Irish hare

Mammals at the Giant's Causeway can be seen just about everywhere if you look closely enough. Rabbits, badgers, foxes, and Irish hares are some of the common land mammals frequently seen.

Looking to the icy waters below the cliffs, though, you'll see a remarkable variety of marine mammals. Sometimes they are difficult to spot, but always close to the shoreline are grey seals, known for their large size and distinctive features. Dolphins, porpoises, and semiaquatic otters are often seen. (A semiaquatic animal lives partly on land and partly in the water.)

Grey Seals

Two seal species live in and around the waters of the North Channel near the Giant's Causeway: the grey seal and the common seal. The grey seal is the larger of the two. In fact, it is the largest land-breeding marine mammal in the United Kingdom.

Males can weigh up to 880 pounds. The grey seal may be bigger than the common seal, but that is not the only distinction between the two species. One striking characteristic of the grey seal is the shape of its nose. The grey seal's nostrils are parallel to each other and their snouts resemble the shape of a pig's nose. The common seal's nostrils are shaped more like the letter *V*. Some people believe this might be how the grey seal got its scientific name, *Halichoerus grypus*. In English that means "hook-nosed sea pig"!

Grey seals spend most of their lives in the water, where they hunt for food. Their diet consists mainly of other sea animals, such as crabs, octopuses, and eels. They are very strong swimmers and can dive down to more than 1,500 feet in search of food. With exceptionally large eyes and very good hearing, a grey seal has little problem finding its next meal in the deep and dark waters.

Fish are everywhere along the coast, and like the marine mammals with whom they share the causeway's North Channel waters, they are not always easy to spot. But they are there! Rock pools host shrimp and crabs along with countless varieties of small fish, such as gobies and blennies. Even eels can be found swimming near the shoreline.

The basking shark is the largest sea animal living in the waters below the cliffs of the Giant's Causeway. It is the second-largest shark in the world, after the whale shark.

In addition to all the fascinating animals, it's easy to be awed by the plant life at the causeway as well. There are approximately two hundred species in the region.

In early summer, the tops of the cliffs are blanketed with wildflowers. The most common of these are bird's-foot trefoil, kidney vetch, sea pinks, and spring squill. On a bright and sunny day in early summer, when these plants cover the landscape, they spread out to look like a huge colorful carpet!

Bird's-foot trefoil

But the causeway is not a very hospitable environment for some species of plants. The soil is very thin along the cliffs and down around the rocks. And the cold winds blowing nonstop have made it necessary for some plants to adapt to the harsh elements. But they have become hardy enough to survive and flourish.

The Basking Shark

Basking sharks are most commonly seen swimming near the causeway in the summer. An adult can be as long as forty feet and weigh in at about 10,000 pounds. It can live to be about fifty years old. One of the most distinctive features of the basking shark is its enormous mouth—sometimes as big as three feet wide! As it swims, most often near the surface of the water, its mouth remains wide open, giving it an ominous look. Not to worry! The basking shark is not interested in eating you, or any other animal! This enormous shark feeds exclusively on microscopic plankton. (Microscopic plankton, often called zooplankton, are tiny, often single-celled organisms that drift in the water.) It swims with its large mouth open to take in and filter the seawater that contains the millions of plankton it needs to consume daily.

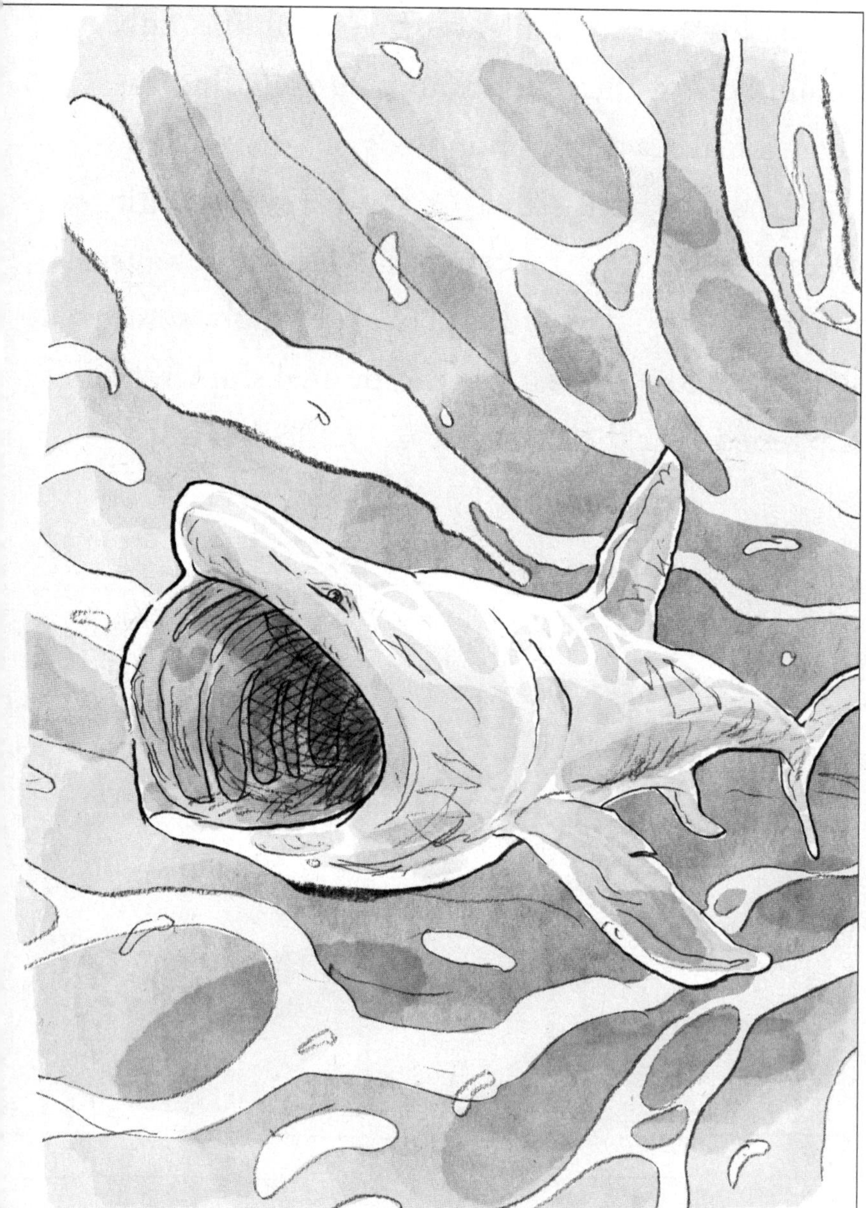

Sharks, fish, and plankton are not the only inhabitants of the rough waters surrounding the Giant's Causeway. For hundreds of years, maybe longer, ships have sailed in the North Atlantic Ocean. Like any rocky coast, the causeway's waters can be a dangerous place. Inevitably, some ships were lost at sea. One exceptional shipwreck happened near the causeway in October 1588.

Rumors of vast treasures aboard the *Girona* were told for hundreds of years. But it was not until 1967 that a team of professional divers located the wreckage of the ship. In it they discovered a huge treasure trove of gold, silver, jewelry, military equipment, and other artifacts. Proof that the rumors were true! It is well worth a visit to the Ulster Museum in Belfast, Northern Ireland, where the *Girona*'s recovered riches are now on display.

The *Girona*

The *Girona* was part of a massive fleet of 130 ships called the Spanish Armada. The ships of the Armada had set sail from Spain early in 1588 to do battle with the British Royal Navy. Their goal was to overthrow Queen Elizabeth I of England. When the Spanish fleet realized they would easily be overpowered, the ships scattered in different directions. Some made the trip back to Spain the long way by sailing north to Scotland and then around the rocky north coast of Ireland. Other ships remained safe far out from the coast in the North Atlantic. But the *Girona* clung to the Irish coastline near the causeway and was not so lucky. One night a violent storm gathered, and the *Girona* crashed into the rocks and was shattered. It quickly sank below the surface. There were 1,300 sailors and soldiers on board, and only nine survived.

CHAPTER 7
What Science Tells Us

The Giant's Causeway became famous when Sir Richard Bulkeley published the account of his visit there in 1693. But geologists believe its forty thousand stone columns and soaring rocky cliffs were created by forces of nature many millions of years ago. (A geologist is a scientist who studies the surface of the earth and what it is made of.)

Geologists believe that until about two hundred million years ago the continents of Europe and North America were attached. They formed a huge part of a supercontinent called Pangaea. The name Pangaea comes from the Greek words *pan* (all) and *gea* (earth), meaning "all of the earth."

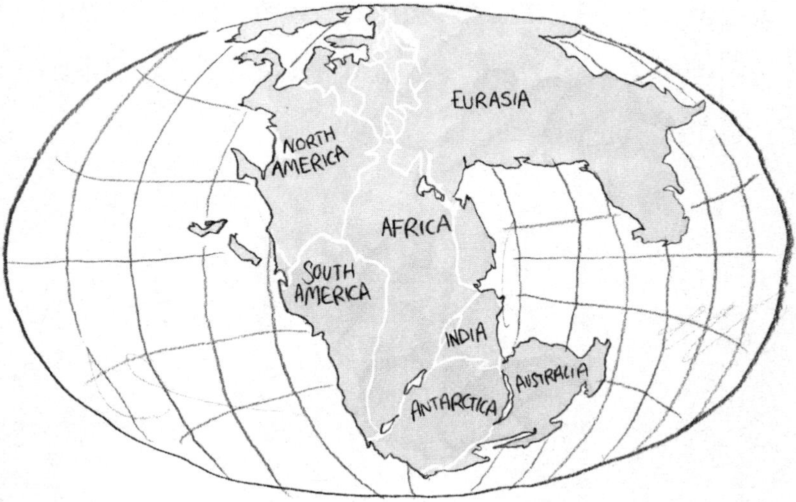

Pangaea

As the earth's continents do today, this enormous ancient continent sat on tectonic plates. These plates were many miles thick and were always moving and shifting, very slowly. As the plates did this, they bumped into each other, moved apart, and drifted past each other. This motion caused Pangaea to split apart. Over many millions of years, new continents were formed, including those we know today as Europe and North America. The constant movement of the tectonic plates caused violent earthquakes and volcanoes. As these earthquakes and volcanic eruptions occurred, mountains, cliffs, and large rock formations were created.

Fast-forward to around sixty million years ago, to the area where the Giant's Causeway is today in Northern Ireland. Deep cracks had formed in the surrounding rocks. These cracks released enormous new volcanic eruptions. The eruptions spewed huge boiling lava flows across the entire area, covering everything in their way. The lava was about 2,000 degrees Fahrenheit, ten times hotter than boiling water! As the lava cooled, it created a kind of rock called basalt, a dark gray or black volcanic rock. Over many years, as the basalt continued to cool, it shrank, and cracks appeared. As the cooling continued, these cracks became larger. Still cooling, they began to come together to form the six-sided columns that make up the Giant's Causeway today. Of course, no process in nature is perfect. Scientists believe that if this one had been perfect, all the columns would have six sides. But some have four, five, seven, eight, or even nine sides. Of all the forty

Basalt rock

thousand columns, most do have six sides, giving the causeway its almost perfect, symmetrical look, just as if it could have been made by people. Or giants!

Over time, nature has created a near-perfect landscape that looks as if humans very precisely carved the geometric stonework.

Rock Columns Around the World

Although the Giant's Causeway is a geologic causeway in myth only (you can't walk across it like a pathway), it is by far the most famous place of its kind. There are other sites around the world that have columns of rock structured very much like the cliffs of the Giant's Causeway. Scientists say they were also formed by volcanic activity many millions of years ago and have hexagonal-shaped columns. They include:

- Devils Tower, Wyoming, United States
- The Organ Pipes National Park, Victoria, Australia
- Basaltic Prisms of Santa María Regla, Hidalgo, Mexico
- Garni Gorge, Armenia
- Isles of Mull and Ulva, Scotland
- The Cliff of Stone Plates, Vietnam

Devils Tower

CHAPTER 8
A Trip to the Giant's Causeway

About seven hundred thousand people visit the Giant's Causeway every year. Most people who make the trip live in nearby countries such as the Republic of Ireland and the United Kingdom (Northern Ireland, England, Scotland, and Wales). Of course, visitors also come from all over the world. The causeway is open all year round, and so is the visitors' center (except for a few days around the Christmas holidays). The busiest times at the causeway are during school vacations and the long summer holiday. The summer months provide the best weather to visit. And it's in the summer when all the plants are on full and colorful display, and when you have the best chances to spot the wide variety of wildlife.

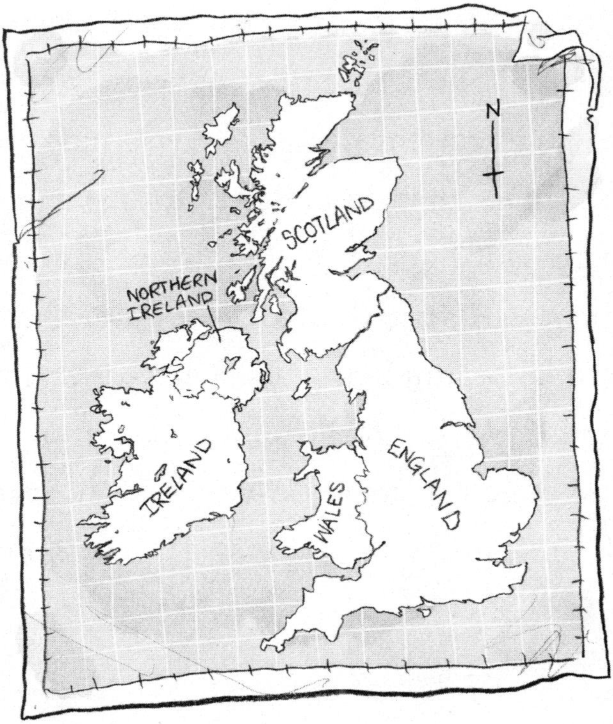

The Republic of Ireland and the United Kingdom

But the causeway is a great place to explore any time of the year, even in winter! There may be more rain and chilly winds leading up to the coldest months, but if you arrive at just the right time, you might catch a glimpse of the giant Finn McCool before he goes into hibernation!

Visiting the Giant's Causeway is an incredible experience. The best place to begin your time there is in its current visitors' center, which opened in 2012. Designed to perfectly fit into the area's dramatic landscape, it is the hub of the visitors' experience. And its builders proclaim that it is built to last a hundred years! The coastline along the causeway is open from dawn until dusk. It's always best to arrive early so you can spend as much time on the site as possible.

Visitors' center at the Giant's Causeway

There is a gift shop at the visitors' center, of course! And there are exhibits on the history of the causeway—its discovery, its growth as a tourist destination, and the incredible plants and animals that make the place their home. Visitors also learn a lot about what scientists have to say about the natural origins of the place. Plus, everywhere you look there are reminders of the story of the giants Finn McCool and Benandonner and the power of the legends that have kept the Giant's Causeway steeped in mystery for centuries.

Seeing the causeway with an official guide is another good way to experience the wonder and mystery of the place. Guided tours are usually highly entertaining and educational, because today's tour guides love the causeway as much as their ancestors did, and they love to tell stories about it. Stories about Finn's exploits are always woven into those about the shifting tectonic plates and the volcanic eruptions. Sometimes it's the other way around. There are four trails that you can take on your own. They are approximately six miles in total and range in degrees of difficulty from easy to challenging. Everyone gets to experience the causeway at their own pace. Many people save as much time as possible to just climb around the causeway rocks and stones, allowing for the opportunity to look high up to the cliffs and down to the rocky coastline, and to take in the great expanse of one of the world's most beautiful places.

It was not until 1962 that the Giant's Causeway was officially opened to the public under the new management of the National Trust, which acquired the causeway the year before. The Trust is responsible for the causeway's management, upkeep, visitor access, and conservation.

The National Trust and a UNESCO World Heritage Site

The National Trust was formed in 1895 to preserve and look after places of natural and historic interest in England, Wales, and Northern Ireland. Today it is one of the largest landowners in the United Kingdom. It owns and manages almost 620,000 acres of land, 780 miles of coast, with hundreds of historical homes and castles, parks, archaeological sites, and nature preserves. Most of these sites are open to the public and are enjoyed by people from all around the world.

In 1986, twenty-five years after the Giant's Causeway was acquired by the National Trust, it was named a World Heritage Site. This designation is given by the United Nations Educational, Scientific, and Cultural Organization (UNESCO) when it considers a site to be of exceptional value. The Giant's Causeway is (so far) Northern Ireland's only World Heritage Site. Quite a distinction!

The Giant's Causeway is infused with Irish history, myth, legend, and mystery. And according to the stories told for centuries, it was built by the heroic, brave, and crafty giant Finn McCool. He wanted to protect his home, family, and fellow countrymen from a Scottish giant said to be even bigger and more menacing than Finn himself.

There are many reasons to believe Finn's story is true. Experiencing the Giant's Causeway up close, while scrambling around the stones and coming upon sure signs that a giant could very well have once roamed here (and may still!) is very different from seeing it or reading about it in books. You can feel the mystery and the possibilities when you're there. And so many of the local people—the guides, shopkeepers, tavern and pub owners—accept the possibilities, believe in the mystery, and want to make sure you do, too.

But not everyone believes the centuries-old myths or the 2015 video footage of Finn. While the video looks like exciting proof that the giant Finn may have once roamed the area, it is not.

It is actually a clever YouTube promotion created by the National Trust to attract tourists to the causeway!

Many people visit the Giant's Causeway and see a beautiful and awe-inspiring natural wonder, a geological phenomenon. They see a place with a sixty-million-year-old history, formed by gigantic volcanoes, hot lava flows, and the slow cooling of the rocks that we step across today. For them, the Giant's Causeway is a remarkable example of the powers and wonder of the natural world.

Two very different points of view, one magnificent place! For centuries, the story of the giants provided the answers. But now science offers a more rational explanation. Was it the hand of a giant who put each rock in place? Or the shifting patterns of geographical circumstances and time? One thing that is certain is that the mystery and the majesty of the Giant's Causeway remains.

Timeline of the Giant's Causeway

mya = million years ago

c. 60 mya	Scientists believe volcanic eruptions created the Giant's Causeway's rock formations
1588	The *Girona*, a ship with the Spanish Armada, is shipwrecked on the coast below the Giant's Causeway
1688	First known written description of the Giant's Causeway by Sir Robert Redding
1693	Discovery of the Giant's Causeway is announced by Sir Richard Bulkeley
1739	Artist Susanna Drury paints first accurate depictions of the Giant's Causeway
1887	The Traill brothers' tram at the causeway opens to the public
1962	The Giant's Causeway opens as a National Trust site
1967	Professional divers locate the *Girona* wreckage and discover its treasure
1986	The Giant's Causeway is named a UNESCO World Heritage Site
2012	A new visitors' center opens
2015	A video appears suggesting a giant was spotted at the causeway
2025	Nearly seven hundred thousand tourists each year visit the Giant's Causeway land formation

Timeline of the World

ya = years ago

c. 65 mya	Dinosaurs become extinct
c. 12,000 ya	Last Ice Age ends
105	Paper is invented in China
1588	Britain defeats the Spanish Armada
1620	The Pilgrims sail from England to North America on the *Mayflower*
1769	James Watt invents the steam engine
1775	The American Revolution begins
1865	The Civil War in the United States ends
1887	Construction begins on the Eiffel Tower in Paris, France
1893	New Zealand becomes the first country in the world to allow women the right to vote
1968	Apollo 8 is the first manned space mission to orbit the moon
2012	Hurricane Sandy hits the northeast United States
2015	The blockbuster musical *Hamilton* premieres at the Public Theater in New York City
2025	Thutmose II's tomb is discovered near Luxor in the Western Valleys of the Theban Necropolis, the first royal Egyptian tomb to be discovered since Tutankhamun's in 1922

Bibliography

***Books for young readers**

*Carroll, Ann. ***The Story of the Giant's Causeway***. Dublin: Poolbeg Press, 2013.

Day, Angélique, ed. ***Letters from Georgian Ireland: The Correspondence of Mary Delany, 1731–68***. Belfast: Friar's Bush Press, 1991.

*Delaney, Rachel. "The Legend of the Giant's Causeway." ***Cricket***, September 2016.

"Giant's Causeway." National Trust. https://www.nationaltrust.org.uk/visit/northern-ireland/giants-causeway.

Groves, Anna. ***Giant's Causeway: National Trust Guidebook***. Swindon, England: History Press Limited, 2016.

*Guillain, Charlotte. ***Finn MacCool and the Giant's Causeway***. North Mankato, MN: Capstone, 2014.

*Karsten, Terri. ***Finn McCool and the Giant's Causeway***. Winona, MN: Wagonbridge Publishing, 2022.

*London, Martha. ***Giant's Causeway***. Minneapolis: Abdo Publishing, 2021.

Osborne-McKnight, Juilene. ***The Story We Carry in Our Bones: Irish History for Americans***. New Orleans: Pelican Publishing, 2020.

Watson, Philip. ***The Giant's Causeway and the North Antrim Coast***. Dublin: O'Brien Press, 2012.